For Jonty – A.S.
For Mum and Dad – E.S.

BLOOMSBURY CHILDREN'S BOOKS
Bloomsbury Publishing Plc
50 Bedford Square, London, WC1B 3DP, UK

BLOOMSBURY, BLOOMSBURY CHILDREN'S BOOKS and the Diana logo
are trademarks of Bloomsbury Publishing Plc
First published in Great Britain 2020 by Bloomsbury Publishing Plc

A catalogue record for this book is available from the British Library

ISBN: HB: 978-1-5266-0858-1; eBook: 978-1-5266-2355-3;
Audio Digital Download: 978-1-5266-2074-3

2 4 6 8 10 9 7 5 3 1

Printed and bound in China by C&C Offset Printing Co. Ltd, Shenzhen, Guangdong

All papers used by Bloomsbury Publishing Plc are natural, recyclable products from
wood grown in well managed forests. The manufacturing processes conform to the
environmental regulations of the country of origin

To find out more about our authors and books visit www.bloomsbury.com
and sign up for our newsletters

ACKNOWLEDGEMENTS

Thank you to my wonderful editor, Elaine Connolly, and to Sharon Hutton, whose idea this was. I also owe a huge debt of gratitude to Dr Richard Thomas (University of Leicester's School of Archaeology and Ancient History), Dr Holly Miller (University of Nottingham) and Professor John Hutchinson (Royal Veterinary College) who generously gave their time to talk to me about their fascinating and painstaking study – the inspiration behind this book. Thank you, also, to ZSL's Archivist, Sarah Broadhurst, and the team in the ZSL library, who kindly allowed me to spend some very special time looking through their Jumbo files. As always, my heartfelt gratitude to Jonty, Flora and Jake for their boundless patience, love, support and interest. Thank you for putting up with me!

BIBLIOGRAPHY

Baker, Samuel W, *The Nile Tributaries of Abyssinia* (1867)

Barnum, P T, *Struggles and Triumphs: Or, Forty Years' Recollections* (1882)

Bartlett, Abraham D, *Wild animals in captivity; being an account of the habits, food, management and treatment of the beasts and birds at the 'Zoo,' with reminiscences and anecdotes* (1898)

Chambers, Paul, *Jumbo, This Being The True Story Of The Greatest Elephant In The World* (2007)

Hagenbeck, Carl, *Beasts And Men: Being Carl Hagenbeck's Experiences For Half A Century Among Wild Animals* (1909)

Johnson, Theophilus, *Personal Recollections of the [London] Zoo during a Period of Fifty Years* (1905)

Jolly, WP, *Jumbo* (1976)

McClellan, Andrew, *Jumbo, Marvel, Myth and Mascot* (2014)

Scott, Matthew, *Autobiography of Jumbo's Keeper and Jumbo's Biography: The Life of "The World's Largest Elephant* (1885)

Sutherland, John, *Jumbo, The Unauthorised Biography of a Victorian Sensation* (2013)

Introduction

Have you ever flown in a jumbo jet, eaten a jumbo hot dog or tackled a jumbo word search on a rainy afternoon?

Even if you haven't done any of these things, the chances are you've heard the word 'jumbo' used to describe something impressively or unusually large. You may even have used it yourself.

But I wonder if you knew that this word became popular thanks to an elephant. Not just any elephant, but a supersized elephant – an elephant who went, of course, by the name of Jumbo.

Born more than 150 years ago in a remote corner of East Africa, Jumbo grew to become – according to popular legend – the largest elephant in the world.

Whatever the truth about his size, we can be certain of one thing: by the time he died, he had become the most famous elephant in the world.

In fact, to this day, many would say Jumbo is the most famous elephant who ever lived.

But how did a baby elephant, who should never have left his far-flung homeland, become an international superstar?

Jumbo and his family in their East African home.

5

Jumbo's early days

Our story begins in 1860 somewhere in the mountainous borderlands of Sudan and Eritrea, which at that time was called Abyssinia.

It was here, in a rugged landscape scoured by torrents of water in the rainy season but parched and dusty in the dry season, that Jumbo began his life.

Within minutes of being born, a blinking baby Jumbo struggled to his feet to take a first mouthful of his mother's milk. Within hours, like all elephant calves, Jumbo was walking – his every movement watched by several pairs of loving eyes. As part of a herd of African elephants, baby Jumbo enjoyed the care and protection of other females as well as that of his mum.

Growing elephants

At first, Jumbo was completely dependent upon his mother's milk, but after a few months he started to eat the usual elephant diet of leaves and branches, as well as grasses, fruit and bark. Growing elephants learn new skills and lessons from their extended family by carefully watching and mimicking them, and Jumbo was no different. It was a schooling that should have lasted for five years but it ended abruptly when Jumbo was just one.

Jumbo learns important skills from his mother.

Jumbo's capture

A year or so after Jumbo was born, an English
explorer called Samuel White Baker and his wife,
Florence, travelled to Africa to search for
the source of the River Nile.

Florence Baker

Samuel White Baker

Their journey took them to Jumbo's remote homeland, where, by the sandy bed of a dried-up river, they came across a group of Hamran tribesmen. The Hamran were famous for hunting and killing elephants, equipped with just a horse, a two-handed sword and a shield. Every part of an elephant, from the skin and fat to the bone and ivory, was valuable to the hunters, either for their own use or for selling on. So Baker was intrigued to see that they had captured two live baby elephants. One of these elephants was Jumbo – although he would not be given that name until he arrived in England some years later.

Tethered alongside the elephant calves were two
young rhinoceroses, three giraffes and several antelope.
The huntsmen explained that they were taking the animals
to a town called Kassala, which was 160 kilometres away.

*There, they would be bought by an Italian businessman called
Lorenzo Casanova, who was hoping to make a small fortune
by selling them on to the zoos and menageries of Europe.*

Zoos, menageries and circuses

In 19th-century Europe and North America the chances of an ordinary person meeting a tiger or lion at some stage in their life were pretty high.

This was all down to a booming exotic animal trade which, in turn, was fuelled by advances in natural science and the spread of empire.

With western countries extending their power and influence around the world, access to weird and wonderful exotic species increased. What's more, people's appetite to see these mind-boggling beasts and birds was greater than ever.

To feed this hunger, zoos open to ordinary members of the public began to spring up in many major cities. The oldest of these still in existence is Schönbrunn Zoo in Vienna. Originally a private collection of wild animals (called a 'menagerie') for the Austrian emperor Franz Joseph I, it opened to all 'decently dressed persons' in 1778.

Zoos around the world

Next came the menagerie at Paris's Jardin des Plantes, which opened in 1794. Things took off in the 19th century when more than a dozen zoos were founded in Europe, including the Zoological Gardens in London, Dublin, Antwerp and Berlin, as well as Amsterdam's Natura Artis Magistra. American zoos got started later with the first one opening in Philadelphia in 1874, followed by others in New York, Atlanta, Washington and Pittsburgh.

Menageries on the move

Meanwhile, for people living outside the big cities, travelling collections of wild animals offered them the chance to see wonders beyond their wildest dreams right on their doorstep.

But as the public grew used to seeing wild animals on display, menagerie owners needed to find new ways of attracting crowds. Their answer was to train these creatures to perform tricks. After all, what could be more exciting than seeing a man attempt to tame a lion, or more extraordinary than watching an elephant trying to balance on a ball?

Circuses soon followed suit. Although traditionally they had only used horses, they began to feature performances from exotic animals too.

Isaac A. Van Amburgh

Isaac A. Van Amburgh, an American animal trainer nicknamed 'the Lion King', is famous for developing the first trained wild animal act in modern times.

As a boy, he started out cleaning the cages of a travelling menagerie before proving himself to be a skilled lion tamer. As well as wrestling with lions, one of his favourite tricks was to place his head inside their jaws. He toured the USA and the UK and even appeared in a pantomime, which was watched by Queen Victoria.

From Africa to Europe

The Bakers saw an underfed and scrawny-looking Jumbo a matter of days after his capture. Without his mother's milk and her love, care and attention, it is little wonder that he was not in a good way.

Although bewildered and frightened, Jumbo was nevertheless strong enough to make the gruelling trek across the desert to Kassala. By this time, the hunters had added even more species to their collection, including cheetahs, jackals, porcupines and ostriches. Remarkably, this slow-moving procession of exotic wildlife finished the journey almost completely unharmed – with only a few animals lost along the way.

The trek to Europe

On arrival in Kassala, the hunters handed the animals over to a grateful Casanova, in exchange for a bundle of dollars. But far from being at an end, Jumbo's ordeal had only really begun. He was about to set out on an epic 10,800-kilometre journey by foot, boat and train to Europe.

The great journey

From Kassala in Sudan, Jumbo marched for six weeks across the scorching sands of the Sahara Desert to the port of Suakin on the Red Sea.

Moving by night to escape the deadly heat, he and his companions covered around 13 kilometres a day. For some of the animals, the challenge proved too much and sadly they did not survive, including Jumbo's fellow elephant calf.

At Suakin, Jumbo was loaded into the sweltering hold of a steam boat, for a 1,300-kilometre ride up the Red Sea to the Egyptian port of Suez.

In Suez, he was transferred on to a train and shuttled 320 kilometres north to the ancient port of Alexandria, on Egypt's Mediterranean coast.

Once in Alexandria, he was hauled by crane – his little legs dangling perilously above the sea – on to a cargo boat bound for the Italian port of Trieste.

After another long train journey, Jumbo reached the German city of Dresden, where Casanova sold the entire collection of animals to the whiskered owner of a travelling menagerie called Gottlieb Kreutzberg, who would sell Jumbo to one of Europe's largest, oldest and wealthiest zoos.

Jumbo's epic journey ended in late 1862, when he finally arrived at Paris's famous zoo, the Ménagerie du Jardin des Plantes.

Jardin des Plantes

The Jardin des Plantes was a large and beautiful public garden on the left bank of Paris's River Seine. It had been created in the 17th century as a royal medicinal herb garden, but by the time Jumbo arrived it was a world-renowned botanical garden containing its own equally impressive zoo.

Bedraggled and standing at around 1.2 metres tall, Jumbo was not much to look at - especially when compared to the adult Asian elephants who already lived at the zoo. So, although he was the only living African elephant in Europe at that time, his arrival did not create much of a stir.

Instead, he was quietly locked away in the Jardin's Rotunda for Large Herbivores, alongside two Asian elephants, camels, giraffes and a hippopotamus.

Castor and Pollux

Not long afterwards, two more African elephant calves joined him - one male and one female. Named Castor and Pollux, they were healthy and bubbling with energy. Their cheeky antics captivated visitors to the gardens and they became known as 'the pets of young Paris'. Poor Jumbo was completely overshadowed.

Meanwhile, conditions in the Rotunda and the rest of the zoo were beginning to bother the French Government. In early 1865, an official investigation declared that the Jardin was desperately overcrowded and ordered it to find new homes for some of its elephants. It did not take long for this news to reach England, where it was warmly welcomed by the superintendent of London Zoo, Abraham Bartlett.

Although London Zoo had plenty of Asian elephants in its collection, it had never got its hands on an African elephant. Now, Bartlett had one within his grasp ...

The large herbivores of the
Jardin des Plantes.

13

Elephant education

There are two species of elephant: African and Asian. As well as living on different continents, they also have many physical differences, which may not be obvious to the untrained eye. Both species of elephant have much in common when it comes to behaviour though.

African elephant

African elephants can live for up to 70 years in the wild.

The African elephant's trunk has two distinct 'fingers' which it uses to pick up and handle objects.

Adult African elephants weigh between 4,000 and 7,500 kilograms.

The African elephant is much larger, with bulls growing up to four metres tall.

All newborn elephants cannot control their trunks very well and must learn how to use them for feeding. With more than 50,000 individual muscle units in the trunk, this is no easy task!

An average adult elephant will drink around 225 litres of water a day – humans are supposed to drink just two litres of water a day!

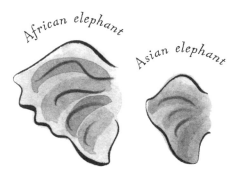

African elephant

Asian elephant

An African elephant's ears look like a map of Africa, while an Asian elephant's ears look like the shape of India.

Elephants spend up to 18 hours a day eating grass, plants, fruit, tree bark and roots.

Unlike most animals, elephants can recognise their own reflection in a mirror.

Asian elephant

Asian elephants live for around 48 years in the wild.

The biggest Asian males measure 3.5 metres at the very most.

Asian males weigh between 3,000 and 6,000 kilograms.

The Asian elephant has only one 'finger' on its trunk.

An adult African elephant can produce up to one ton of poo a week.

All elephants love mud baths. The mud helps cool them down and is an excellent sunscreen. It also provides relief from biting insects.

A Jumbo deal

Bartlett wasted no time in making his move,
offering to exchange a grumpy Indian rhinoceros for
one of the Jardin's three African elephants. The French
drove a hard bargain but eventually agreed to strike a deal.

So, it was on a warm June day in 1865 that Jumbo found himself standing at a railway station on the edge of Paris. This unremarkable spot was where Jumbo would meet the man destined to become the most important presence in his life: his friend and carer, Matthew Scott.

Matthew Scott

Matthew Scott was an awkward character with few, if any, human friends.

His fellow keepers at London Zoo found him stubborn, touchy and often downright rude. However, he had an understanding of the natural world that set him apart from all of them – a gift he had shown from a young age.

Early beginnings

Scott was born on the Knowsley Hall estate in Lancashire, UK, in 1834. Knowsley was home to the Stanleys, a rich, aristocratic and influential family, also known as the Earls of Derby.

The 13th Earl of Derby, Edward Smith Stanley, was fascinated by nature and had spent years creating his own private wildlife park.

The wildlife keeper

When he was just ten years old, Scott went to work in the Earl's aviary, looking after his parrots. Five years later, he was promoted to keeper of the Earl's deer and antelope.

Scott stayed there until 1851, when the Earl died and his son took over the estate. Preferring politics to parrots, the new Earl set about auctioning off his father's animals. Before he did so, however, London Zoo was allowed to choose what it wanted from the collection. The Zoo selected some of the antelope in Matthew Scott's care and asked if they could have Scott too!

A new life at the Zoo

So, at the age of seventeen, Scott said goodbye to his family and journeyed south to start a new life as a junior assistant keeper at London Zoo in Regent's Park.

The work was tough and the pay was low but Scott thrived in his new role. Impressed by what he saw, Abraham Bartlett put Scott in charge of caring for the Zoo's latest and most exciting addition – its first African elephant. Scott's initial task was to travel to Paris and bring Jumbo back to London.

Scott leads Jumbo through the streets of London.

From Paris to London with Scott

If Bartlett had seen his new elephant before sealing the deal with the Jardin des Plantes, he might have had second thoughts.

When Scott met Jumbo on the train platform in Paris, he declared he had never seen a more wretched-looking creature. But while others may have given up on Jumbo as a lost cause, Scott was determined to do all he could to help him.

As a seasoned traveller, Jumbo must have thought nothing of the short boat and train journey from France to London. However, the final stretch of the trip was more of a trial. Alighting at London's Waterloo station, he and Scott had to complete their journey to the Zoo on foot. It was an uncomfortable trek for Jumbo, whose hoofs had become rotten and misshapen due to neglect.

A new home for Jumbo

On their arrival, Scott settled a grateful Jumbo into his own stable, where he was given a comfortable, clean bed. Used to being alone, it was a pleasant surprise for Jumbo when, instead of leaving for the night, Scott lay down next to him. In fact, from this time onwards the two would rarely be apart.

Over the following weeks Scott watched over Jumbo day and night. Using lotions and oils, he healed the young elephant's sores, removed his scabs and scraped and rasped his feet. Slowly but surely, Jumbo's health was restored.

Jumbo and Scott rest in the elephant den.

Naming Jumbo

Along with his new home came a new name – Jumbo. Nobody knows exactly how he got it but many theories have emerged. Some think that he was named after *Mumbo Jumbo,* an African spirit. Others think that Jumbo came from the Swahili word, *Jamba,* meaning hello; or that it came from the Zulu word, *Jumba,* meaning a large packet. The mystery remains unsolved. But whoever did name Jumbo would surely never have imagined that this little orphaned elephant from East Africa would earn a place in dictionaries the world over.

London Zoo

The world's first scientific zoo, London Zoo, opened for business in 1828.

For almost 20 years, entry was restricted to members of the Zoological Society of London who visited it for scientific study. But in 1847, in need of more money, the Zoo opened its gates to the paying public.

Seen in scientific circles as a rival to the Jardin des Plantes menagerie, London Zoo proudly boasted a great many 'firsts'. These included the world's first-ever public aquarium and reptile house and Europe's first living hippopotamus since Roman times. Its first African elephant was soon to become yet another jewel in its crown.

21

Zoo life

By early 1866, Jumbo was fighting fit and ready to play a more active part in zoo life.

A cautious Bartlett took things slowly at first, only letting him venture into a paddock outside his den. The next step was to take him on walks around the Zoo. To Bartlett's relief, Jumbo was not remotely bothered by the crowds. In fact, he revelled in the attention, staying relaxed and cheerful amid the hustle and bustle of excited visitors.

But the strains of his stint in the cramped Jardin des Plantes had taken their toll on his mind. Jumbo hated being locked up and would show his distress by repeatedly charging at the doors of his den. He also ground his tusks down on his den walls and they never grew very big.

Damage to the den

Jumbo himself, however, was big. He had grown to 1.8 metres tall – about the length of a bed – and was capable of inflicting some serious damage on his surroundings. The carpenters and blacksmiths were kept busy with constant repair work and, in the summer of 1866, the doors and walls of Jumbo's den were fitted with steel-plating to protect them from his outbursts.

Jumbo remained peaceful during the day, when he was not shut inside. So, with his bad behaviour limited to night-time hours, Bartlett trusted Jumbo enough to let him start carrying people on his back.

An African elephant called Alice arrived at London Zoo in September 1865 and became Jumbo's 'wife', which thrilled Scott and the Victorian public. But the pair were never really anything more than friends who enjoyed the occasional bath together.

Jumbo returns a young boy to his mother.

The ultimate ride

Training began in earnest and, by the end of 1866, Jumbo was giving rides to children around the Zoo grounds.

As he waited patiently, the excited youngsters would hand over their pennies and scramble aboard his back using a set of wooden steps. Once they were sitting securely on a leather saddle, Scott would guide Jumbo around the Zoo, using a collar and lead. In an age before cars and rollercoasters, a ride on an African elephant would have been a thrill that children would remember forever.

The following year, Jumbo was strong enough to carry more people. The saddle was replaced with a howdah - a large wooden seat designed to hold up to six adults or eight children. Instead of walking alongside Jumbo, a proud Scott sat astride his neck, gently encouraging the children to sit quietly so they would not fall off.

An amazing encounter

On one occasion Jumbo was giving a ride to a group of young people, when he came to an abrupt halt. Looking down, Scott saw that a boy had run into their path, with his frantic mother in hot pursuit. Completely unruffled, Jumbo used his trunk to pick the little boy up gently by his waist and lay him softly on the green grass.

It was stories such as this that won Jumbo a special place in the public's heart. No trip to London Zoo was complete without a ride on *'the* elephant at the Zoo'. Among the thousands of children who rode on his back were Queen Victoria's children and the young Winston Churchill. Even Theodore Roosevelt - the future US president - was said to have ridden on Jumbo as a young boy.

But Jumbo continued to lead a double life. By day, he would entertain the crowds. But as night fell, his tantrums would return, becoming more damaging and dangerous the larger and stronger he grew.

Illness and miracle cure

*Just as Bartlett was wondering how to solve the problem of
Jumbo's rages, an unfortunate turn of events put a stop to them.*

In December 1867, Jumbo became dangerously ill. Regular visitors to the Zoo noticed the change in Jumbo, who had become too weak to participate in his usual routine. It seemed as though Jumbo's final hour had come.

Bartlett and the Zoo's veterinary surgeons were completely stumped by the mystery illness and believed he was beyond cure. But Scott announced that he would be able to help the elephant and asked to be left alone with Jumbo to work his magic.

*Scott tends to
the unwell Jumbo
over Christmas.*

A hope for Christmas

Although it was the depths of winter, Scott moved back into Jumbo's freezing den. A stove was brought in to stave off the cold as he stayed there day and night, hoping for his own Christmas miracle.

As the new year arrived, stark and unpromising, it brought with it some remarkable news. Jumbo was on the mend! When asked how Scott had restored Jumbo's health, he teasingly replied 'with bucketfuls of whisky'.

Jumbo and Scott

Jumbo's comeback came as a huge relief to Bartlett.
How long would the peace last though?

During their triumphant battle with death, Jumbo and Scott had formed an unbreakable bond. Jumbo's devotion to Scott meant he would take instruction from no one else.

But, for now at least, there was calm in the African elephant den. Jumbo's temper remained in check and his chemistry with Scott saw his popularity go from strength to strength. To the delight of visitors to London Zoo, the elephant and his keeper would clown around like a comedy duo. When Scott wasn't looking, Jumbo would steal his hat. A 'furious' Scott would then work himself into a fit of rage that would last until Jumbo replaced the hat delicately on his head.

Sweet treats for Jumbo

Jumbo would charm onlookers with his tricks too – stretching his trunk into the crowd and helping himself to sips of tea from people's cups or pinching food from their hands. As a reward for entertaining them, the crowd would feed Jumbo with handfuls of sticky buns.

Jumbo and Scott entertain crowds at London Zoo.

Jumbo's mysterious rages

For over a decade, life continued as normal for Jumbo – or whatever normal is for an African elephant living in London. Each day, from 2 p.m. until 6 p.m., he would trundle his passengers patiently around the Zoo. When the Zoo had gone to bed, he and Scott would sometimes share a glass of whisky before Scott broke into song, accompanied by a trumpeting Jumbo.

But in 1881, the peace was shattered. Jumbo's night-time rages returned and he began attacking the doors, walls and windows of the Elephant House again. Now 21, Jumbo was over three metres tall and weighed five tonnes, as heavy as three cars. So his powers of destruction were far greater than before.

A decision for Bartlett

Jumbo's violence was a cause of great concern for Bartlett. He knew that adult male elephants would sometimes become troublesome and dangerous. This condition – known as musth – occurs when male elephants are ready to mate. Bartlett had heard of people being killed by elephants in musth and he knew things could end badly.

So, with a heavy heart, he asked the Zoo council to buy him a powerful gun, along with permission to shoot Jumbo should the worst come to the worst.

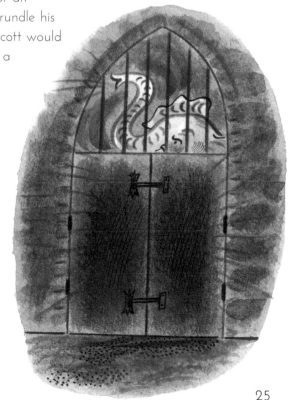

Desperate to find another solution,
Bartlett received a well-timed offer.

P.T. Barnum

On 13th December Bartlett received a telegram which simply read: 'What is the lowest price you can take for the large male African elephant?'

The telegram was signed by 'Barnum, Bailey and Hutchinson', the owners of America's world-renowned 'Greatest Show on Earth'. Phineas Taylor Barnum, or P.T. Barnum for short, had made his fame and fortune by carving out a glittering career in entertainment. He had started out in 1835 by paying $1,000 (around $28,000 in today's money) for the right to put a '161-year-old' woman on public display. It was claimed that she had been a nursemaid to the first president of the United States, George Washington. The woman's name was Joice Heth — she was actually half her advertised age and she was a slave. The entire story was, of course, a whopping lie. But none of this bothered Barnum. Why care about the facts when the public were prepared to pay handsomely for a show? The whole business was completely outrageous but it made Barnum a quick buck and gave him a taste for more of the same.

A million wonders

Barnum went on to manage travelling acts and run a museum of 'a million wonders' in New York, where his exhibits included a bearded lady, a 2.4-metre-tall giantess and a performing dwarf called General Tom Thumb.

In 1870, Barnum started his own circus, which he boldly named 'P.T. Barnum's New and Greatest Show on Earth'. Ten years later, he joined forces with a rival circus run by James Bailey and James Hutchinson. Each year, Barnum would send his agents to Europe to discover fresh attractions. Nothing but the very biggest and the best would do for 'The Greatest Show on Earth'. So it is little wonder that the majestic Jumbo was at the top of Barnum's shopping list.

On 25th January 1882, an announcement appeared in The Times newspaper ...

JUMBO SOLD

JUMBO   JUMBO

THE GREAT AFRICAN ELEPHANT

Barnum, the American showman, has bought for the sum of £2,000, the largest male African elephant, which has for many years formed one of the principal attractions in the Gardens of the Zoological Society in the Regent's Park.

The purchase has been made upon the understanding that the animal is to be removed and shipped to America at the risk of the purchaser. To those who know, the size, weight, and strength of this ponderous creature (certainly the largest elephant in Europe), the undertaking is one of serious difficulty and not unattended with some danger.

Elephant Bill

Despite the warning, few could have guessed just how difficult the removal of Jumbo from London Zoo would prove to be.

Eager to claim his prize, Barnum sent his most experienced elephant handler to London without delay. William Newman – known as 'Elephant Bill' – arrived in England in early February and set about organising Jumbo's passage to the USA.

Leaving London Zoo

The plan was to build a large wooden box on wheels, rather like a horse box, that would transport Jumbo from Regent's Park to Millwall Dock. From there, the box would be hoisted on to the Persian Monarch, *a large steamship due to set sail for New York on Sunday, 19th February.*

Aware of the close relationship between Jumbo and his keeper, Barnum hoped that Scott would travel to the USA with the elephant and stay for a short while to help him settle.

On Saturday, 18th February, Scott made his way to Jumbo's den. This was the day that Jumbo would be boxed up and pulled by a team of horses to Millwall. But Jumbo was going nowhere. He point-blank refused to enter the box. After an hour or more, Newman's patience had run out and he ordered chains to be put around Jumbo's feet, legs and neck. If Jumbo was not going to enter the box voluntarily, he would be dragged in. By this time, visitors had begun arriving at the Zoo. A crowd gathered around the elephant house, watching in fascination as the pantomime unfolded.

As night closed in, it became clear that Newman needed a change of tack.

A Jumbo operation

Plan B was to walk Jumbo the 14 kilometres to Millwall Dock.

Newman's hope was that by the time Jumbo got there he would be too tired to put up a fight. A more cooperative Jumbo could then be led into the box and winched on to the ship.

At dawn the next day, Scott led Jumbo towards one of the Zoo's exits. News of the previous day's excitement had travelled fast and, despite the early hour, a large and curious crowd was waiting outside. Jumbo did not disappoint them.

Jumbo won't leave

No sooner had he stepped foot outside the Zoo gate, than he let out a 'sad moan'. Wrapping his trunk around Scott in an enormous hug, he stopped, lay down and refused to budge. Eventually, when it became clear that all hopes of catching the ship were lost, Scott led him back to his den.

The crowd – who had been deeply touched by the sorry scenes – cheered in triumph and relief. They were not alone in their feelings. Jumbo's plight was about to capture the hearts and minds of the British public in quite an extraordinary way.

Jumbomania

*Presented with all the ingredients for a blockbusting story,
the British press were quick to act. The next day, newspapers
carried emotional accounts of Jumbo's brave stand.*

On Tuesday, 21st February, *The Times* published an angry letter from a member of the Zoological Society of London expressing his disgust at the sale and his horror at Jumbo's 'pathetic and almost human distress'.

The floodgates open

Newspapers across the country were swamped with letters from furious readers demanding that something be done to save 'the children's pet' from his fate.

Meanwhile, letter after letter landed on Abraham Bartlett's desk – scolding him for his decision, begging him to change his mind and even threatening him with death.

It was not just adults who wrote. A whole school presented the Zoo with a petition to save Jumbo. Children fired off appeals to Queen Victoria, as well as to P.T. Barnum himself, begging him to reconsider his purchase.

Visitors flock to the Zoo

At the same time, ticket sales for London Zoo soared. On Monday, 27th February, the Zoo had just over 8,500 visitors. But on the previous Monday, there had only been about 1,500. Numbers continued to rise as men, women and children flocked through the gates to say their farewells to Jumbo.

Songs were written and sung in his honour by the musical stars of the day. Shops sold a fantastic assortment of Jumbo souvenirs, including Jumbo bonnets, umbrellas, jewellery, ornaments and even Jumbo perfumes.

The more dedicated Jumbo fans sent parcels of treats to him. Pastries, a giant pumpkin, wine, beer and a dozen oysters all arrived at the Zoo. One bride even sent him a slice of her wedding cake.

Barnum responds

Barnum was delighted with the hullabaloo Jumbo caused. When first told of Jumbo's refusal to leave the Zoo, he had replied: 'Let him lie there for a week if he wants to. It is the best advertisement in the world.'

And when the editor of one national newspaper asked him to name his price for cancelling the sale, Barnum replied: 'Fifty-one millions of American citizens anxiously awaiting Jumbo's arrival. £100,000 would be no inducement to cancel purchase.'

His words were published in newspapers up and down the country – no doubt causing much spluttering into British tea cups.

A new plan

In the meantime, Newman and Bartlett had been working out what to do next.

Firstly, they made the giant wooden crate stronger and narrower, to ensure that it would support Jumbo more effectively. Then they cooked up a plan to familiarise Jumbo with it.

They placed the box in a large hole so that its floor was level with the ground. Both ends were then removed – making it into a wooden tunnel. The idea was that Jumbo would be walked through the tunnel regularly to get him used to being inside the box. Once he was ready, they would secure him inside with chains, close up the ends and haul the box out of the pit using a set of metal rails.

Zoo workers build a new box.

Jumbo makes a stand.

An unexpected obstacle

This time it would not be Jumbo who would thwart Newman's plans.

On Monday, 6th March, a letter was published in *The Times* announcing that a group of Fellows from the Zoological Society of London were mounting a legal challenge to Jumbo's sale. All of this was a step too far, even for Barnum. Afraid that his scheming would backfire, he hired the best lawyers available to fight his corner. The British and American nations watched and waited to see which way the case would go.

After much nail-biting back and forth, the judge declared the sale valid. Jumbo would be going to the USA.

But the judgement had come too late for Jumbo to take his place on the *Egyptian Monarch*. The next ship, the *Assyrian Monarch,* would sail on 25th March leaving plenty of time to get Jumbo boxed up.

Another ship is booked

On Saturday, 4th March, Scott introduced Jumbo to the newly altered box. Unsurprisingly, Jumbo was no more impressed by this version than he had been by the last. After gingerly inspecting it with his trunk, he refused to step foot inside.

Once again, an angry Newman ordered Jumbo back to his den. Yet he was optimistic enough to book him a place on the *Egyptian Monarch*, which was due to sail in five days.

Newman orders Jumbo back to his den.

Jumbo is boxed up at last.

Time to go

As the Zoo's visitor numbers swelled to an extraordinary 24,000 on Monday, 13th March, Newman made a breakthrough. He had identified the cause of Jumbo's stubborn behaviour: it was Matthew Scott.

Newman was convinced that Scott had been secretly commanding Jumbo to misbehave and, after raising his suspicions with Bartlett, the pair hatched a plot to outwit the keeper. Bartlett ordered Scott to take a holiday, explaining that Newman and Jumbo needed time to get to know one another.

He also reminded Scott that P.T. Barnum had invited Scott to travel with Jumbo to the USA. This did the trick. Scott begged Bartlett not to send him away and promised to do his best to get Jumbo to behave.

So, the following morning, with the help of Scott, Jumbo was safely boxed up.

London to New York:
The second epic journey

*In the small hours of Thursday, 23rd March, 1882, Jumbo
began the second epic journey of his short lifetime.*

A team of ten horses pulled Jumbo through the streets of London. Despite the foul weather and the early start, thousands had turned out along his route to St Katharine Dock to wave their goodbyes. On arrival, the box was loaded on to a barge by a large crane and floated downstream to Millwall Dock. A small fleet of rowing boats followed on behind carrying more well-wishers.

The next day, Jumbo was hoisted on to the *Assyrian Monarch* – a large steamship built to carry passengers and cargo between London and New York. One of the ship's decks had been cut away to ensure there was enough room for Jumbo's giant box. With the special cargo safely stowed, a grand lunch party was held in Jumbo's honour. And so, with cheers ringing in their ears, Jumbo and Scott set sail for the New World.

Across the Atlantic

The crossing to New York took a little over a fortnight. Despite the noise of the machinery and the rolling of the ship, Jumbo caused no trouble at all. In fact, Scott wrote that he became 'quite the sailor', once he had found his sea legs. No doubt a drop of whisky helped them both along the way.

At last, on the morning of Saturday, 8th April, the ship sailed into New York Harbour. 'Jumbo seemed to be delighted,' wrote Scott. 'He trumpeted out his joy, as much as to say: Ah! Mr Scott, we are at last in the land of the free and the home of the brave.'

A new home in the New World

Whipped up into a frenzy by Barnum's slick marketing machine, 10,000 men, women and children were waiting for Jumbo on the dockside.

They watched in awe and fascination as what Barnum had billed as 'the largest and heaviest elephant ever seen by mortal man, either wild or in captivity' was lifted ashore and towed through the streets of Manhattan to his new home in Madison Square Garden.

When Jumbo finally stepped out of his cramped box, onlookers were amused to see him carefully test the ground with one foot, as if to confirm it was solid enough to bear his weight. Once satisfied, he lay down and rolled on to his back, revelling in his new-found freedom after almost three weeks inside.

According to Scott, such was his joy, that he 'twined his trunk around me in an ecstasy of delight'.

Jumbo in the USA

*Thousands flocked daily to see Barnum, Bailey and Hutchinson's legendary
spectacle in Madison Square Garden, featuring exotic animals,
acrobats, jugglers, fire-eaters and countless other acts.*

Barnum put Jumbo on display straightaway. Unlike the circus's Asian elephants, Jumbo was spared the torment of being forced to perform tricks, stunts and punishing routines. Other than being the show's prize exhibit, his only roles were to give rides to children and to take pride of place in its grand parade on the track surrounding the three circus rings. Barnum was thrilled with Jumbo's reception, later announcing that increased ticket sales during his first two weeks at the show had more than paid for his purchase and the expense of getting him to the USA.

With a whole touring season ahead of them, this was a promising start!

The wonder of Jumbo
Jumbo proved himself to be the perfect promotional tool. Everywhere you looked, his name and picture appeared. You could buy Jumbo cotton thread, Jumbo soap and Jumbo polish. He was even used to advertise pills to ease constipation, ladies' suspenders and luxury oysters.

Touring North America

After 30 days in Madison Square Garden, Barnum, Bailey and Hutchinson packed everything up and set off on their grand tour of the USA and Canada.

The touring season was relentless – packing in up to 100 rail journeys and two or three shows per day. At each stop, Jumbo was met by hordes of adoring fans. Even those who could not afford 50 cents to see the show would happily pay 25 cents just to see him in his pen.

Barnum continued to fuel the nation's curiosity by refusing to allow anyone to measure Jumbo's height and he urged the public to see Jumbo before he grew too large to travel. Newspapers declared him to be a towering four metres high – more than half a metre taller than he had been when he left London.

A winter break

After clocking up more than 20,000 kilometres, it was time to rest for the winter. Despite the upset of travelling and the frustration of being confined to his stall in the winter months, Jumbo's rages didn't return. He even made a new mischievous friend – a dwarf elephant called Tom Thumb, nicknamed 'the Clown'.

As king of the show, Jumbo travelled in a specially built railway van, called his 'Palace Car'.

An incredible rescue

In 1883, faced with the choice of returning to London or remaining in the USA, Scott decided to stay put.

Later that year, Jumbo would repay his friend's loyalty. One evening, as the pair were awaiting the next performance, they heard the thunderous sound of stampeding feet. To Scott's horror, some of the circus elephants were charging towards him. Convinced he was about to be crushed to death, Scott found himself being lifted out of harm's way by Jumbo's trunk. Gently placing Scott between his legs, Jumbo kept Scott safe until the keepers had regained control. He had saved Scott's life!

Brooklyn Bridge

In the spring of 1884, Jumbo and Scott found themselves centre stage in another Barnum publicity stunt – this time on New York's brand-new Brooklyn Bridge.

Spanning the East River from Manhattan to Brooklyn, it was the longest suspension bridge in the world. However, days after it opened, someone fell down the steps and, in the panic to get off the bridge, 12 people died.

It was not long before rumours began to swirl about its safety. Who better to quash those rumours than Jumbo, 'the largest living beast'? On 17th May, 1884, a crowd of 10,000 curious New Yörkers held their breath as Jumbo and Scott stepped proudly on to the bridge. Following on behind them were 21 elephants and 17 camels. Scott had grave concerns that if Jumbo became agitated, his great weight would bring the bridge crashing down. But with his trusty keeper by his side, Jumbo remained calm, pausing only to look quizzically at the steamboats rushing along under his legs.

The stunt went without a hitch – Jumbo had delivered for P.T. Barnum once again.

Jumbo's last days

With Jumbo's fame and Barnum's fortune snowballing, the 1885 circus season began with more pizzazz than ever before.

A fourth circus ring was unveiled and there was even talk of taking the whole show on tour to Australia and Europe.

The schedule ran smoothly and, as autumn arrived, the performers were turning their minds to their well-deserved winter break. On 15th September, the circus rolled into St Thomas, a small town in the Canadian province of Ontario. As usual, the wagons were unloaded and the showground set up on a site not far from the railway yard.

A peaceful evening

After the final performance, the staff packed up the tent and began walking the animals down the railway track to the waiting carriages. It was a warm evening and all was quiet. With no trains scheduled on the line for some hours yet, the circus team could take their time.

Jumbo and Tom Thumb were the last to leave the showground. As they neared the goods yard, Jumbo and Scott were looking forward to their beds.

But just as they were picking their way along the final stretch of track, Scott heard something that made his stomach lurch. From not too far down the line came the low but unmistakable rumble of a freight train. It was coming swiftly towards them and it was on the same track. On one side of the elephants was a steep embankment and on the other were the circus carriages.

They were trapped.

A chance of survival

A desperate Scott urged Jumbo and Tom Thumb to climb down the embankment but the terrified elephants flatly refused. As the train thundered towards them, their only choice was to run forwards. If they could reach the end of the circus carriages and dive off the track before the freight train caught them, they would be saved. Scott frantically shouted at the elephants to run for their lives. Bewildered and panicking, Jumbo charged ahead, his trunk held high, trumpeting as he ran.

Meanwhile the hapless driver of Special Freight Number 151 had seen what lay in his path. Horrified, he shifted the engine into reverse and blasted the train's whistle three times – a signal for his brakemen to apply the brakes.

As the train bore down on them, a desperate Scott flung himself off the track and down the slope. Then, with a deafening screech of brakes and a cascade of sparks, the train struck Tom Thumb, sending him flying down the embankment. Finally, with an almighty crash, it hurtled headlong into Jumbo and came to a shuddering halt. Amid the smoke and the hissing steam, Scott crawled back up to the track to find Jumbo lying quietly on his side. He was still breathing but even the stately Jumbo – the largest elephant in the world – was no match for a freight train.

A heartbroken Scott held his trunk and talked gently to him as Jumbo slipped silently away.

Life after Jumbo

*Jumbo's legacy continues to touch the lives of
people and animals around the world.*

In the 1800s, his remarkable life helped ignite an interest in elephant behaviour that has seen the way we now think about these highly intelligent and emotionally complex creatures completely transformed.

We now understand that to remain happy and healthy, elephants need three key things: space to roam, the right food and the companionship of their own kind. Above all, we now recognise that a circus or a cramped zoo is no place for an elephant.

The show goes on

But P.T. Barnum was not quite ready to say goodbye to Jumbo.

'Jumbo dead is worth a small herd of ordinary elephants,' he declared and lost no time in employing the finest taxidermist to preserve, stuff and mount Jumbo's skin. It should come as no surprise that Barnum gave instructions for Jumbo's skin to be stretched – making Jumbo look even larger than he had been in real life. Meanwhile, Jumbo's skeleton was reconstructed so that it could be exhibited alongside his stuffed hide.

A touching reunion

Jumbo continued to tour with the circus for another four years, along with his 'wife' Alice, whom Barnum had brought over from England. On being reunited with Jumbo, Alice tenderly touched his face with her trunk, before letting out a mournful groan.

There were no lengths, it would seem, to which Barnum would not go to squeeze the last dollar from Jumbomania.

The end of an era

Scott toured with Jumbo and Alice until the end of 1886, when his employment with the circus ended. He disappeared completely from history in 1887, with no trace of his final days recorded anywhere.

Over the next few years, Jumbo's star began to fade, and in 1889 Barnum cut his losses and donated the stuffed hide to Tufts University in Boston. Jumbo's skeleton was sent to the American Museum of Natural History in New York, where it remains carefully preserved to this day.

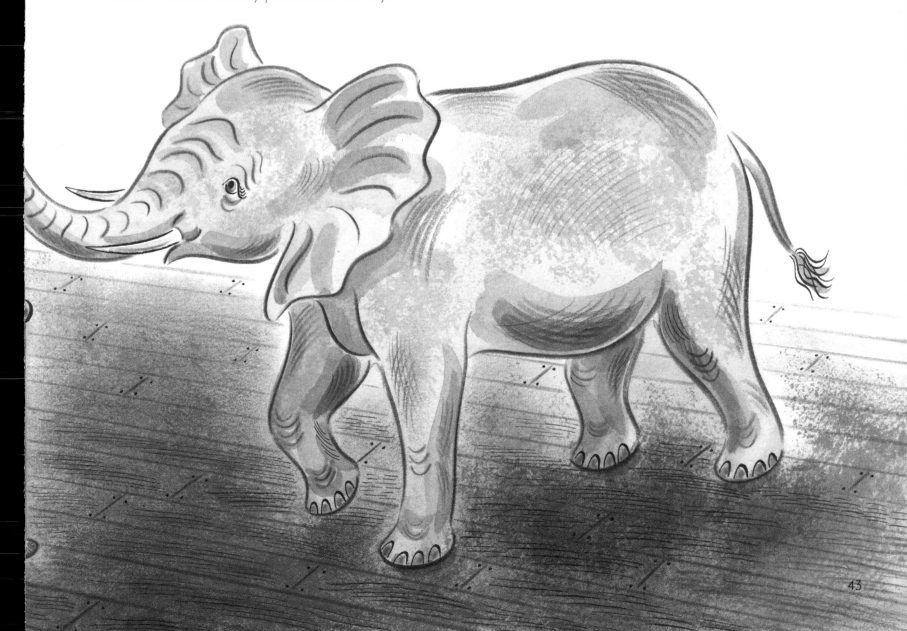

Jumbo's bones

In 2017, for the first time ever, the American Museum of Natural History let scientists carry out detailed tests on Jumbo's bones.

Using painstaking techniques, the scientists – from the Universities of Leicester and Nottingham and London's Royal Veterinary College – were able to shed light on some of the mysteries surrounding Jumbo's life.

Causes of the rages

Bartlett was certain that the reason for Jumbo's rages was musth. However, the experts concluded that Jumbo may actually have been suffering from terrible toothache.

Throughout its lifetime, an elephant will have six sets of molars. As a tooth wears out, another one pushes forward to replace it. In the wild, elephants eat a lot of wood and bark – which grinds down their teeth. However, Jumbo's teeth were not getting worn down by his soft zoo diet. So new teeth were trying to grow before the old ones had fallen out. The upshot was that Jumbo's teeth were badly misshapen and in the wrong position. What is more, the sticky buns and sugary treats fed to Jumbo became trapped in the gaps between his teeth, causing painful decay and infection.

Jumbo's bones and joints also show signs of injury and disease.

Although he was a young elephant in the prime of life, he had the body of one twice his age. This was partly down to a poor diet that was not giving him the right range of nutrients. But it is also likely that years of carrying thousands of children and adults on his back had taken their toll.

Jumbo's outbursts were not just the result of physical pain.

The experts believe they could also be explained by stress. From the moment of his capture in Sudan, Jumbo had been deprived of the regular company of other African elephants. Like humans, elephants are highly social and form deep relationships with their friends and family. In his 21 years, Jumbo had been through a lot of tough experiences and, throughout it all, he had been alone. Even the loyal presence of Matthew Scott and his occasional contact with Alice could not compensate for everything he had lost or provide everything he needed.

Jumbo's size

By measuring Jumbo's bones, the scientists concluded that Jumbo was around 3.2 metres tall at shoulder height.

This is a long way off the four metres Barnum liked to claim he was. However, Jumbo was still 20 per cent larger than he should have been at his age and he was still growing. We can only imagine how tall he would have become if he had been fed and treated correctly, and had he lived to a ripe old age.

The sanctuaries

In 2016, 131 years after Jumbo's death, the Ringling Brothers and Barnum & Bailey Circus – the successor to Barnum's Greatest Show on Earth – finally stopped using elephants in their performances.

As other circuses follow suit, sanctuaries for retired and rescued captive elephants have sprung up around the world. They include the Elephant Nature Park in Thailand's Chang Mai, the Elephant Conservation Centre in Laos, which rescues elephants from the logging industry and tourism, and Sri Lanka's Elephant Freedom Project.

Some of these sanctuaries – like the Elephant Sanctuary in the US state of Tennessee – cover thousands of acres, allowing their residents to wander at their will and experience what it is like to be a wild elephant for the first time in their lives. It was here that two elephants, called Shirley and Jenny, who had briefly performed together in a circus, were reunited after 22 years apart. They remembered one another and formed a powerful bond, like you would see in the wild.

Elephant protection

This change in attitudes toward elephant welfare goes far beyond the world of circuses. Many zoos that once kept elephants for their curiosity and entertainment value are now at the forefront of efforts to protect them.

The menagerie at the Jardin des Plantes no longer owns any elephants. London Zoo stopped offering elephant rides in 1960 and, in 2001, 170 years after the first one arrived, the final elephant left Regent's Park for good. The Zoo now runs conservation programmes around the globe. These projects work to protect elephants threatened by illegal poaching for their ivory tusks and to shield them from the destruction of their natural habitat. Other zoos around the world – from Australia to North America – are doing the same.

Although these changes came too late for Jumbo, he continues to speak to us over the centuries, reminding us how far we have come and how far we have yet to go. Even in death, Jumbo remains larger than life.

  # Jumbo's journey

North America

10. St Thomas, Ontario
9. New York

Europe

8. London Zoo
7. Jardin des Plantes, Paris
6. Dresden
5. Trieste

Africa

320 km
4. Alexandria
3. Suez
1,300 km
500 km
2. Suakin
1. Kassala

Abyssinia to Paris

Jumbo began life on the borderlands of modern-day Sudan and Eritrea

1. After being captured, he was marched across the desert to a town called Kassala, in modern-day eastern Sudan.

2. From Kassala, he trekked for six weeks across the Sahara Desert to the port of Suakin in modern-day Sudan on the Red Sea.

3. After a steam boat ride up the Red Sea, Jumbo arrived at the Egyptian port of Suez.

4. Jumbo was transferred on to a train and shuttled north to the ancient port of Alexandria, on Egypt's Mediterranean coast.

5. On arrival in Alexandria, Jumbo was lifted on to another boat which would sail him across the Mediterranean Sea to the port of Trieste in modern-day Italy.

6. After Trieste, Jumbo travelled by train to the city of Dresden in modern-day Germany.

7. Jumbo arrived at Paris's Jardin des Plantes in 1862.

Paris to London

8. In 1865, Jumbo travelled by train, boat and foot from Paris to London Zoo.

London to New York

9. In 1882, Jumbo was transported by horse-drawn carriage, barge and steam boat to New York.

10. Jumbo travelled by train around the USA and Canada with P.T. Barnum's circus. His final stop, marking the end of his life's journey, was the small Canadian town of St Thomas, Ontario.